GRACE
is *Amazing!*

Written By Lynnette Maynor

Illustrated by Judy Plumley

Book Design & Formatting by Starry Eyes Media
www.StarryEyesMedia.com • 1-800-889-8343

For Him...

As blessings flow onto us from God's hand,
let us be sure to kiss it.

I am sincerely thankful to God for granting me the privilege to write this book.

I would like to thank illustrator, Judy Plumley, for the beautiful hand painted pictures, and Starry Eyes Media for their excellent graphic design. Most importantly, I am thankful for their willingness to go the distance. I am also very thankful to everyone who has contributed in any way to help make this book possible.

On a personal note, I would like to express my thankfulness to God for gracing us with three special gifts: our Grandsons, Drake, Brody and Grayson.

Last, but not least, I would like to thank you for reading this book.

Love and blessings to you,

*L*ynnette Maynor

Grace is so amazingly wonderful;
given to us in love,
it's every good and perfect gift,
that comes from the Father above!

These gifts we call favor or blessings.
They come from God's own hand.
He showers them upon us.
In grace we always stand.

There's grace for our sickness and sadness;
grace for our worries and fears,
grace that forgives when we make a mistake,
as God helps us and dries up our tears.

God gives us the grace to be happy;
grace to have laughter and fun,
grace that brings gladness, love, peace and joy,
seems our grace journey has begun!

$\mathcal{L}$et's open a few grace packages
and take a look inside,
to see these amazing gifts,
that God does so richly provide!

$\mathcal{T}$hese gifts were bought for us
a long, long time ago.
Jesus paid for them on the cross
because He loves us so.

$\mathcal{L}$et's start with the gift of love;
the one that's wrapped in red,
reminding us of Jesus' blood,
upon the cross He shed.

$\mathcal{T}$his gift is most amazing;
the reason we have grace!
Because of God's love, He gave His son Jesus;
Who chose to take our place.

"...God is love." - I John 4:7

"For God so loved the world that He gave His only begotten Son, that whoever believes in Him should not perish but have everlasting life." - John 3:16

"The grace of the Lord Jesus Christ, the love of God, and the fellowship of the Holy Spirit be with you all." - II Corinthians 13:13

Here's the calming gift of peace.
We don't have to be anxious or afraid.
This gift soothes and comforts us;
causing our worries to fade.

Jesus is the Prince of Peace;
Who is always there,
giving us peaceful rest,
as we give Him all our care.

His peace is like a soft warm blanket;
comforting us inside.
No matter what's going on,
in Him we can calmly abide.

"A child (Jesus) is born to us! A son is given to us!
And he will be our ruler. He will be called, Wonderful
Counselor, Mighty God, Eternal Father, Prince of
Peace." - Isaiah 9:6

"When I am afraid, I will trust in You." - Psalm 56:3

Jesus said, "...Peace I leave with you, My peace I give to
you..." - John 14:27

"May God give you more and more grace and peace
as you grow in your knowledge of God and Jesus our
Lord." - II Peter 1:2

Let's look at the gift of joy!
How exciting to see,
a gift that causes us to rejoice;
filling our hearts with glee!

God gives us joy and gladness!
He puts a smile upon our face!
He fills our mouth with laughter!
He's our happy place!

There's a beautiful place we see God's grace;
at the table when spread,
with delicious food and drinks,
as God gives us our daily bread.

This shows how He takes care of us.
It's good to let Him know.
We are thankful for everything.
We can tell Him so.

"God satisfies the thirsty and fills the hungry with good things." - Psalm 107:9

"It is good to give thanks to the Lord, to sing praises to the Most High." - Psalms 92:1

How special it is to give!
We're privileged to be a part;
in bringing our love gifts to God,
those that come from the heart.

When we bring our gifts to Him,
whether large or small,
He opens the windows of heaven,
and lots of blessings begin to fall!

Every time we give to Him
much more is returned.
He's the greatest giver!
Nothing from Him is earned!

Let's open the gift of healing;
in case we have this need.
We can ask God to heal us.
We don't have to beg or plead.

Because of God's grace and kindness
He hears His children's prayers.
He's always ready to help us;
showing how much He cares.

When Jesus walked upon the earth
He healed all who'd believe.
The Bible says He doesn't change;
so healing's ours to receive.

It only takes a little faith.
God says that's all I need.
I pray in faith, believing;
if only the size of a mustard seed.

"...I am the Lord who heals you." - Exodus 15:26

"...Jesus went about all the cities and villages, teaching in their synagogues, preaching the gospel of the kingdom, and healing every sickness and every disease among the people." - Matthew 9:35

"Jesus Christ is the same yesterday, today and forever." - Hebrews 13:8

"...If you have faith as a mustard seed...nothing will be impossible for you." - Matthew 17:20

At times we are not perfect.
We may make mistakes and fall.
That's when God forgives us.
His grace covers them all!

He reaches down and picks us up;
and says everything's okay.
Please accept my gift of forgiveness.
My mercies are new everyday!

Sometimes Satan brings wrong thoughts,
and he just won't go away.
We tell him to go in the name of Jesus!
He's not allowed to stay!

That's when he must leave.
He has to obey our command.
Since we belong to Jesus,
in Him we take our stand.

God tells us to do so.
He gives us the right;
to stop every thought of the enemy,
putting him to flight.

This gift is called authority.
We have the right to use His name.
Since we belong to God's family,
we're one in Him the same.

We are to have a mind like Christ
in everything we do.
As we keep our minds on Him
our thoughts are lovely and true.

The greatest wonder of God's amazing grace,
which He so carefully planned,
He showed us His love when He gave His Son, Jesus,
so in His grace we can stand.

Jesus, the most beautiful picture of grace.
The cross makes it plain to see.
He loved us to death, as He laid down His life,
to save us and set us free.

He is the only way to heaven.
He is the door.
He died on a cross and rose from death
to remove our sins forevermore.

To have this free gift you must believe.
This is what you can say.
Dear God, I have sinned and I am sorry.
I receive Jesus today.

Jesus said, "I am the door." - John 10:9

"...If you confess with your mouth the Lord Jesus and believe in your heart that God has raised Him from the dead, you will be saved." - Romans 10:9

"...As many as received Him (Jesus), to them He gave the right to become children of God, to those who believe in His name..." - John 1:12

"For by grace you have been saved through faith, and that not of yourselves; it is the gift of God, not of works, lest anyone should boast..." - Ephesians 2:8-9

Once you receive Jesus as Savior
your graced in every way!
You're loved, accepted and forgiven;
with tremendous blessings each day!

With salvation being the greatest,
His grace gifts far outweigh,
anything we can imagine,
in this life and in heaven someday!

Heaven is full of surprises!
Won't it be exciting to see;
God in all of His glory,
and the gifts waiting for you and me?

Jesus said, "In My Father's house are many mansions...I go to prepare a place for you." - John 14:2

When John saw into heaven he said, "The city (of Heaven) was made of pure gold, as pure as glass. The foundation stones of the city walls had every kind of jewel in them..." - [Revelation 21:18-19]

"...Now God's home is with men. He will live with them, and they will be His people. God himself will be with them and will be their God. He will wipe every tear from their eyes. There will be no more death, sadness, crying, or pain. All the old ways are gone. (God) The One who was sitting on the throne said, "Look! I am making everything new!" - [Revelation 21:3-5]

God is so good and kind. He graces us in many ways. The greatest way He blessed us, is by giving His perfect Son, Jesus, to take away our sins, so we can go to heaven one day. Sin is anything wrong we may think, say or do that hurts God. Since no sin can be in heaven, it has to be taken away. The Bible says Jesus took our sins in His body to the cross, where He suffered, bled and died in our place. His blood continues to wash away the sins of everyone who believes in and receives Him as their Savior.

You can receive Jesus now. Here is what you can say to God...

Dear God,

I know I have sinned, done wrong things, and I am sorry. I believe Jesus died on the cross and rose from the dead to take away my sins. I invite Jesus into my life now.

Thank you for forgiving me and washing away all my sins with the blood of Jesus. Thank you for receiving me into your family. I'm so glad you love me! I love you too!

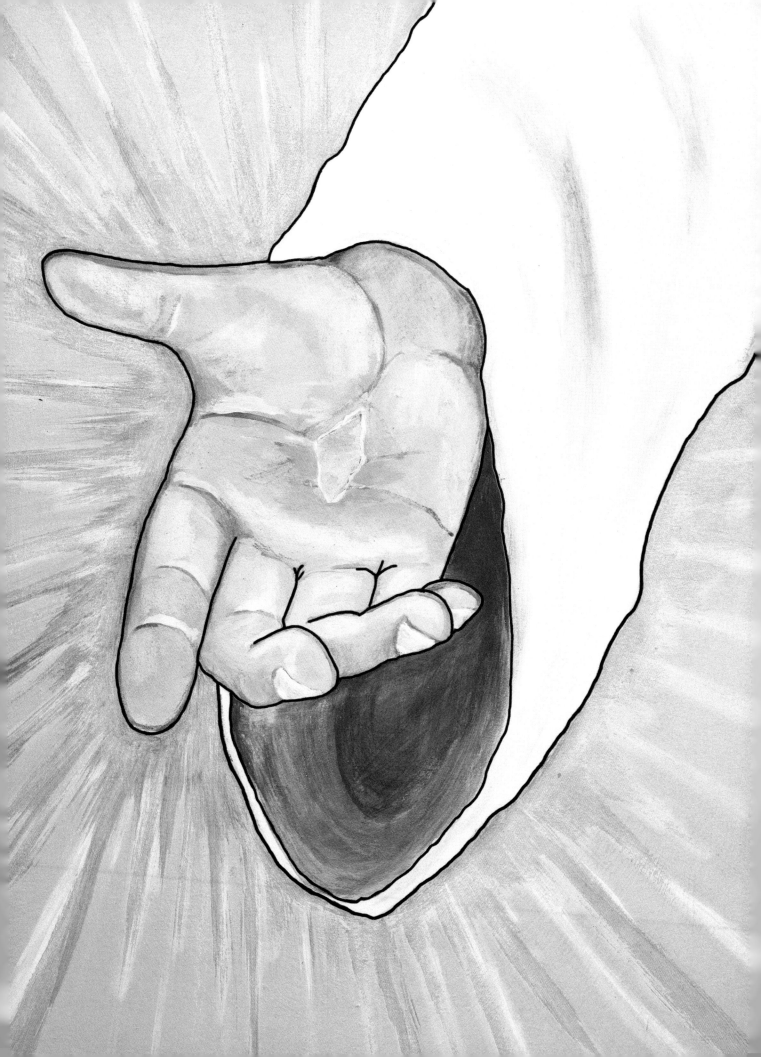

$\mathcal{I}$t's so wonderful to belong to God's family, knowing He will always be there for His children! He is a friend who sticks closer than a brother! I'm so glad His Holy Spirit now lives inside to guide, comfort, and help me. Every day I want to read His words from the Bible and pray, so I can know Him better and live the life He has planned for me.

"...There is a friend who sticks closer than a brother." - Proverbs 18:24

Jesus said, "I have called you friends..." - John 15:15

"I will never leave you nor forsake you." - Hebrews 13:5

"...Grow in the grace and knowledge of our Lord and Savior Jesus Christ..." - II Peter 3:18

"[God's Spirit of truth]...will guide you into all truth..." - John 16:13

God gives us more
than we can hold!

God's Grace
is Amazing!

Additional
Scripture References

"For all have sinned, and come short of the glory of God." - Romans 3:2

"For God so loved the world, that he gave his only begotten Son, that whosoever believeth in him should not perish, but have everlasting life." - John 3:16

"…As many as received Him (Jesus), to them He gave the right to become children of God, to those who believe in His name…" - John 1:12

"Christ died for our sins…He was buried…He rose again the third day according to the scriptures." - I Corinthians 15:3-4

"You are not redeemed with corruptible things…but with the precious blood of Christ." - I Peter 1:18-19

"Jesus…bore our sins in His own body on the tree…" - I Peter 2:24

Jesus said, "I am the way, the truth, and the life: no man cometh unto the Father, but by Me." - John 14:6

"If we confess our sins, He is faithful and just to forgive us our sins, and to cleanse us from all unrighteousness." - I John 1:9

Made in the USA
Columbia, SC
04 December 2020